Garfield takes the cake

BY: JIM DAVIS

BALLANTINE BOOKS · NEW YORK

Library of Congress Catalog Card Number: 82-90219
ISBN: 0-345-32009-3

Manufactured in the United States of America

First Edition: October 1982

40   39   38   37   36   35   34   33   32   31

GARFIELD EATING TIPS

1. Never eat anything that's on fire.

2. Never leave your food dish under a bird cage.

3. Only play in your food if you've already eaten your toys.

4. Eat every meal as though it were your last.

5. Only snack between meals.

6. Chew your food at least once.

7. Avoid fruits and nuts: after all, you are what you eat.

8. Always dress up your leftovers: one clever way is with top hats and canes.

9. A handy breakfast tip: always check your Grape Nuts for squirrels.

10. Don't save your dessert for last. Eat it first.

DO YOU KNOW WHAT I LIKE ABOUT CATS, GARFIELD? YOU'RE SO DOCILE

11-24

ROWR!

I HATE TO BE PEGGED

JIM DAVIS © 1980 United Feature Syndicate, Inc.

11-25

OH NO!

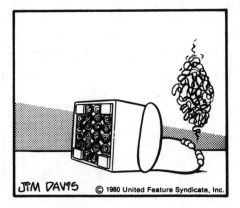

JIM DAVIS © 1980 United Feature Syndicate, Inc.

11-28

THIS TABLE IS DUSTY

ACHOO!

TWENTY YEARS FROM NOW I'LL LOOK BACK ON THIS AND LAAAAUGH

11-29 © 1980 United Feature Syndicate, Inc.

BOY, AM I BORED

JIM DAVIS   12-1

GOOD MORNING, GARFIELD. IT'S ANOTHER DAY JUST LIKE ANY OTHER DAY. ISN'T IT GREAT?

SOME PEOPLE CONFUSE BOREDOM WITH SECURITY

© 1980 United Feature Syndicate, Inc.

I NEED A CHANGE

JIM DAVIS   12-2

MAYBE I'LL TAKE UP A HOBBY. MAYBE I'LL LEARN A NEW LANGUAGE. MAYBE I'LL PARTICIPATE IN A SPORT

MAYBE I'LL STAY BORED. IT TAKES LESS EFFORT

© 1980 United Feature Syndicate, Inc.

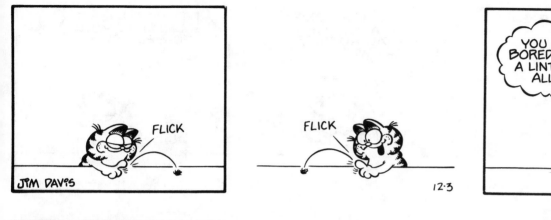

FLICK

FLICK

JIM DAVIS

12-3

YOU KNOW YOU'RE BORED WHEN FLICKING A LINT BALL BECOMES ALL-CONSUMING

© 1980 United Feature Syndicate, Inc.

EVERY DAY IT'S THE SAME BORING FOOD, SAME BORING PEOPLE, SAME BORING ROUTINE...

RRRR

JIM DAVIS

12-4

ROWR!

FFFT!

...SAME BORING FIGHTS

© 1980 United Feature Syndicate, Inc.

I THINK IT'S TIME YOU MET A LADY CAT, GARFIELD

JIM DAVIS

12-15

AND IF YOU'RE NOT SURE WHAT TO DO ON A DATE JUST WATCH ME IN ACTION SOMETIME

I HAVE

MAKE AN INNUENDO, GET SLAPPED. MAKE A SUGGESTION, GET SLAPPED. MAKE A MOVE, GET SLAPPED

© 1980 United Feature Syndicate, Inc.

JON SAYS THIS AFTER SHAVE IS SUPPOSED TO ATTRACT WOMEN

12-16

JIM DAVIS

GALLOP
GALLOP
GALLOP
GALLOP

DARN... WRONG SPECIES

© 1980 United Feature Syndicate, Inc.

GOBBLE!
GOBBLE!
GOBBLE!

1-2   JIM DAVIS

WHERE'S YOUR DINNER?!! WHERE'S MY DINNER?!!

ONCE MY EATING GAINS MOMENTUM IT'S HARD TO SHUT DOWN

© 1981 United Feature Syndicate, Inc.

OKAY, WHO ATE MY SOCKS?

JIM DAVIS

GARFIELD!!

THE GUY'S SOME KIND OF A PSYCHIC!

1-3   © 1981 United Feature Syndicate, Inc.

OH NO! I FEEL A NAP ATTACK COMING ON. BUT THE MOVIE'S ALMOST OVER. I MUST STAY AWAKE!

1-9

JIM DAVIS

© 1981 United Feature Syndicate, Inc.

Z

BOY, WHAT A GREAT NIGHT'S SLEEP

YAWN

JIM DAVIS

1-10

HEY, GARFIELD. LET'S GO JOGGING

Z

© 1981 United Feature Syndicate, Inc.

MY FEET! WHERE ARE MY FEET?!

JIM DAVIS

2-9

MAYBE I COULD STAND TO LOSE A POUND OR TWO

© 1981 United Feature Syndicate, Inc.

GARFIELD, I WOULDN'T SAY YOU'RE FAT...

JIM DAVIS

BUT YOU HAVE MORE CHINS THAN A HONG KONG TELEPHONE DIRECTORY!

2-10

© 1981 United Feature Syndicate, Inc.

BRINNNNG!

JIM DAVIS 2-23

I LOVE TO WAKE UP EARLY

THE EARLIER YOU SET YOUR ALARM, THE LONGER YOU CAN OVERSLEEP

© 1981 United Feature Syndicate, Inc.

IT'S YAWN AND CRICK TIME

JIM DAVIS 2-24

YAWN

CRICK!

© 1981 United Feature Syndicate, Inc.

© 1981 United Feature Syndicate, Inc.

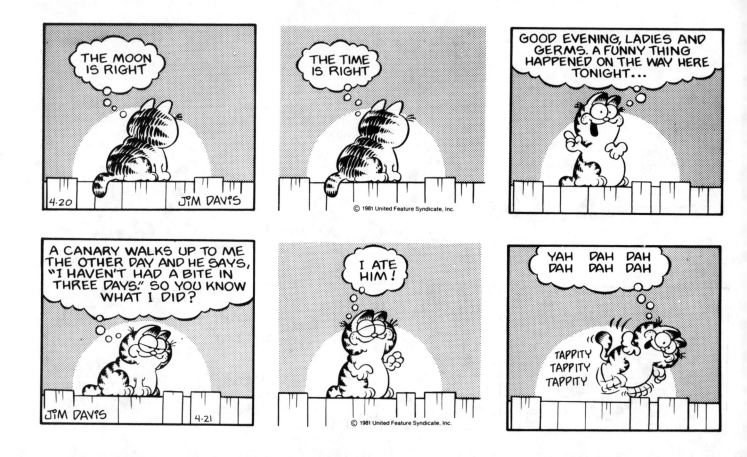

GARFIELD CHARACTERS THAT DIDN'T MAKE IT

When I initially designed GARFIELD, these concepts
never made it off the drawing board. Maybe they could all be
brought back in a strip called ROGUES' GALLERY.

JIM DAVIS